Animals with Backbones

Keith Pigdon

What do these animals have in common?
All of these animals have backbones.
Animals with backbones are called **vertebrates**.

2

3

Fish are vertebrates.
Their bodies are covered with scales.
Fish live in the water.
Fish have gills.
The gills let the fish breathe underwater.

Sea horse

Angel fish

4

Eel

What other vertebrates have gills?

Amphibians are vertebrates.
Amphibians have gills when they are young.
They hatch from eggs and live in the water.
Amphibians grow lungs when they are older.
Then they live on the land.

Salamander

Toad

6

Frog

What other vertebrates live on the land and in water?

Reptiles are vertebrates.
Many reptiles live on the land and in water.
Reptiles have lungs.
They can't breathe underwater.
Most reptiles lay eggs.

Turtle

Alligator

8

Snake

What other vertebrates lay eggs?

Birds are vertebrates.

Birds lay eggs.

Most birds fly.

Their bodies are covered with feathers.

Birds live in hot and cold places.

Ibis

Eagle

10

Robin

What other vertebrates live in hot and cold places?

Mammals are vertebrates.
Mammals live in hot and cold places.
Their bodies are covered with fur or hair.
Mammals don't lay eggs.
They give birth to their young.
Mammals feed their young milk.

Dog

Sea lion

12

Bear

13

These animals all look different.
But they are all alike in one important way.
They all have backbones.
All of these animals are vertebrates.

Reptile

Fish

Amphibian

14

Bird

Mammal

15

Glossary

amphibians   animals that have gills and live in water when they are young, and grow lungs and live on land when they are older

backbone   a column of bones down the middle of the back that supports an animal's body

birds   animals that lay eggs and have feathers; most birds can fly

fish   animals that have gills, and live and breathe in the water

gills   the parts of the body that let some animals breathe underwater

lungs   the parts of the body used to breathe air

mammals   animals that give birth to their young and feed their young milk

reptiles   animals that have scales and breathe with lungs; many reptiles live on land and in water

vertebrates   animals that have a backbone